ANCIENT GREECE

by Robert Nicholson

Editorial Consultant: Patsy Vanags,
British Museum, London

Scholastic Canada Ltd
123 Newkirk Road, Richmond Hill, Ontario, Canada L4C 3G5

Copyright ©Two-Can Publishing Ltd, 1992
Text copyright © Robert Nicholson, 1992
Design by Belinda Webster
Edited by Claire Watts and Liz Wise

First published in Great Britain in 1992 by
Two-Can Publishing Ltd
27 Cowper Street
London EC2A 4AP

Published in Canada in 1992 by
Scholastic Canada Ltd.
123 Newkirk Road
Richmond Hill, Ontario
Canada L4C 3G5

Printed and bound in Hong Kong

Canadian Cataloguing in Publication Data
Nicholson, Robert
    Ancient Greece

Canadian ed.
Includes index
ISBN 0-590-74380-5

1. Greece - Civilization - To 146B.C. - Juvenile
literature. I. Title.

DF215.N53 1992   j938   C92-093341-6

Photographic credits:
Ancient Art and Architecture Collection: p.9(r), p.10, p.11(b), p.16, p.19(t);
The Bridgeman Art Library: p.22(t), p.23(b); ET Archive: p.13(t), p.30(l);
Werner Forman: p.7; Michael Holford: p.9(t,c), p.11, p.15, p.19(b), p.20,
p.22(l), p.23(t), p.24, p.30(t); Toby: p.20(b), Zefa: p.30(b)

Illustration credits: Maxine Hamil: cover, p25-29; Mike Allport p3-24

Contents

All words marked in **bold** can be found in the glossary.

Italy

ADRIATIC SEA

Pindus Mountains

Macedonia

Mt Olympus

Troy

AEGEAN

Delphi

Athens

Peloponnesus

Olympia

Sparta

IONIAN SEA

SEA OF CRETE

Crete

Home of Minotaur

MEDITERRA

The Greek World

The civilization of ancient Greece lasted from about 2000 BC to 200 BC. The peak came during what is called the classical period, between 500 BC and 400 BC. At this time, Greeks controlled the mainland and islands we now know as Greece, as well as the land around the eastern end of the Mediterranean which was settled by Greek traders and farmers.

During this time the Greek people lived in many separate city states. Each city state was based around one city, and included the surrounding countryside. Greek thinkers and artists wanted to make these fair and beautiful places to live. Many of their ideas and inventions influenced Europe and its peoples as they developed. From there, Greek ideals have spread all over the world.

Asia Minor

Land conquered by
Alexander the Great

Rhodes

Cyprus

The Greeks travelled
to these areas to
farm the land.

N E A N   S E A

Alexandria

Egypt

Greek Lands

Mainland Greece and the islands which surround it are hot and dry with many high mountains and steep-sided valleys. Its hills and valleys were once heavily wooded, but by the classical period many of the forests had been cut down. The Greek mainland is surrounded almost entirely by water.

Farmland was scarce because of the rugged countryside, and was mainly near the coast and in sheltered valleys, where the most important crops were wheat, barley, grapes and olives. However, the Greeks were skilled sailors and keen traders which meant that they could import food.

Small village communities were very isolated from one another because of the high mountains and steep valleys. There were very few roads, and most journeys had to be made on foot.

▲ Because overland travel was so difficult, the Greeks travelled whenever possible by sea. Stormy seas and rugged coasts meant that this could be very dangerous. Sailors had no compasses and had to navigate by the stars.

▶ Olive trees growing on a dry, rocky hillside.

City States

Greece was not one united country as it is today. Instead it was made up of separate city states. A city state, or **polis,** was based around one city, and included all the surrounding farms, villages and houses.

Athens was the city of education and learning. Athenian philosophers, politicians and artists were famous throughout Greece. Around 300,000 people lived in the city and the surrounding countryside.

Sparta was Athens' greatest rival. Sparta was famed for the strength of her army. There were many wars between the two cities, each of which was trying to gain control of the whole of Greece.

▼ This is the ancient city of Athens. The Acropolis, which means high city, was easy to defend in times of war. The main temple of the city, the Parthenon, was built on this hill.

The Peloponnesian War

The rivalry between Athens and Sparta eventually led to the Peloponnesian War (431 to 404 BC). Sparta attacked Athens first, fearful of the city's growing power. After many triumphs and setbacks, Sparta won the war, but both states were weakened after 27 years of fighting.

▶ Their only defence was their bronze shields.

▲ This vase painting shows Greek soldiers, armed with shields, spears and swords.

▲ Greek soldiers used a variety of weapons: spears, javelins, daggers, arrows and slingshots.

Citizens and Slaves

In Greek cities, there were groups of people with different rights and different roles to play in society. The two main groups were **citizens** and **slaves**.

Citizens could own property and take part in politics and the law. In Athens and some other cities, most adult men were citizens. In Sparta, only men from the richest families had citizens' rights. Women were not citizens, even those of important families. They had few or no rights, and had little power outside their homes.

Slaves could not be citizens either. Slaves were usually captured prisoners of war. They were owned by the people they worked for, and were bought and sold like property. Some lived quite comfortably with the families they worked for. Others lived in miserable conditions or toiled in mines until they died. Most slaves were paid for much of the work they did. If they saved enough money, they could buy their freedom.

▲ Each Greek city minted its own coins, stamped with its own symbol, such as this owl of Athens.

▲ This vase painting shows women slaves drawing water from a fountain.

Government

Many of the city states of Ancient Greece were **democracies**. In a democracy, the decisions about government were made by councils of ordinary citizens. Only adult men were entitled to be citizens. Some city states, however, were ruled by rich and powerful landowners, supported by armies.

In Athens, all citizens voted to decide how the city was run, what taxes to pay, whether to go to war and so on. Poor workers were even paid a full day's wages to attend the government assemblies. There were no separate politicians or lawyers in Athens. All free men took part in politics and legal affairs.

▲ Jurymen used discs such as these to vote in courts of law. Hollow discs indicated 'guilty', solid 'not guilty'.

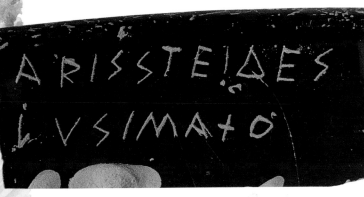

▲ Citizens could vote to banish politicians by writing their names on these pottery fragments, called **ostraka**.

Philosophers and Scientists

The ancient Greeks were very curious about themselves and the world around them and made many important advances in science, learning and art. Great thinkers were known as **philosophers** no matter what subject they studied. The word philosophy comes from the Greek words for 'love of wisdom'. Philosophers tried to find out how the universe worked, why people were good or evil, and how people should live their lives.

Many Greek discoveries provide the foundations of modern knowledge and beliefs. Greeks studied the stars and discovered that the earth floated freely in space, turning on its own axis. They also correctly predicted eclipses of the sun. Sometimes they were wrong. Ptolemy, a Greek scholar, thought the earth was the centre of the universe.

Most new ideas were never used for solving practical problems. Metal-working techniques, for example, were still primitive; they were never developed enough to make tools that could take advantage of the advances made in science.

Famous Philosophers

● **Hippocrates** (around 460 – 377 BC)
Hippocrates founded a medical school, where he practised scientific medicine instead of magic or religion. He taught the value of knowing how the body works.

● **Aristotle** (384 – 322 BC)
Aristotle examined living things in nature. He also wrote on many subjects, including politics, and invented a method of thinking called logic.

● **Socrates** (around 469 – 399 BC)
Socrates, one of the first great philosophers of classical Greece, taught the value of questioning common beliefs in order to find new ideas and explore new truths.

▲ Bust of Socrates.

● **Plato** (around 427 – 347 BC)
Plato founded a school for philosophers called The Academy where he taught Aristotle. His famous books are *The Republic* and *Dialogues*.

◄ The Greek philosopher Eratosthenes calculated the circumference of the earth by measuring the angle of the sun at Alexandria in northern Egypt, and measuring the distance from there to Syene in southern Egypt, where the sun was overhead at noon. His figure for the circumference was correct to within 320 km.

Soothsayers and Oracles

The Greeks had many gods and goddesses who usually represented a particular aspect of life, such as love or war. Most of them were believed to live on **Mount Olympus.** The Greeks told stories about their gods, in which they fought and loved, and were angry or jealous just like men and women.

Many of the gods had temples where priests or priestesses performed rituals in their honour. Gods were often honoured by **sacrifices**. Usually these were just gifts of food and wine but on big feast days or festivals, many animals were sacrificed.

The Greeks looked to the gods for anwers to all their problems. For simple questions, such as "Should I marry this man?" they would go to a **soothsayer**, who would study the weather or the insides of a sacrificed animal to find the gods' answer.

For more complicated questions, such as "how should we defeat our enemies?" a visit to an **oracle** was necessary. At Delphi, the famous oracle, a priestess called the Pythia would go into a trance and give a reply which had to be interpreted by priests. It cost a lot of money to consult Pythia.

The Olympic Games

The Greeks believed that having a fit body was a way of honouring the gods. Games were held all over Greece in honour of different gods or festivals. The Olympic Games were held once every four years in honour of Zeus. They lasted five days, and people came from all over Greece to compete in athletic events. Wars were even postponed for three months so that people could travel safely to see the games. The events included boxing, wrestling, discus-throwing, javelin-throwing, long-jump, running and chariot races.

Important gods

ZEUS and **HERA** were the king and queen of the gods.
POSEIDON was the brother of Zeus and the god of the sea.
DIONYSOS was the god of wine.
ARES was the god of war.
HERMES was the messenger god.
APOLLO was the god of music and healing.

▲ Aphrodite, the goddess of love.

◀ Athene, the goddess of wisdom and of Athens itself, is born from the head of Zeus.

15

Theatre and Writing

Even today, ancient Greek literature is still being read, and plays are still performed.

Poetry was the earliest form of Greek literature. Homer was the first major poet. He composed long poems telling the stories of the adventures of heroes and gods. His best known poems are the *Iliad* and the *Odyssey*.

The Greeks were the first civilisation to record their history as it happened. Before this, people passed on the news of events by word of mouth and their stories quickly became exaggerated.

▲ In comedies, costumes were padded, making the actors look grotesquely funny.

Drama

Drama developed from songs and dances to honour the gods. Theatres were built next to temples, and plays were an important part of religious festivals. There were two sorts of plays: tragedies and comedies.

Tragedies were sad and violent tales of love and war. They often retold old myths about the gods and related these to the lives of people. Comedies made fun of politics, religion and important local people.

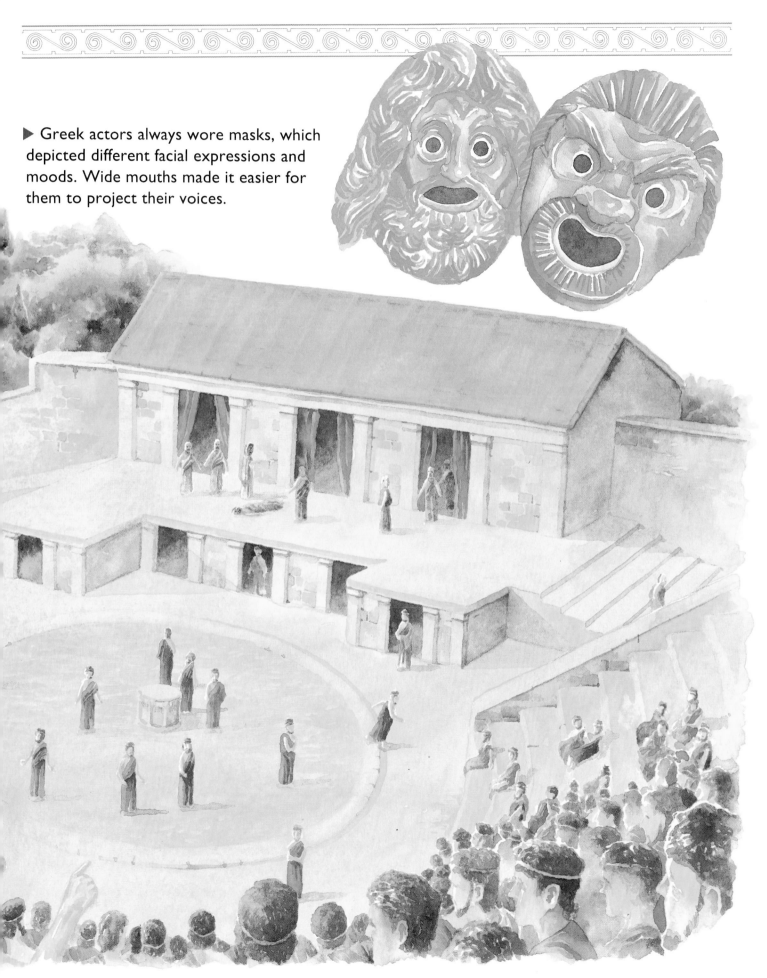

▶ Greek actors always wore masks, which depicted different facial expressions and moods. Wide mouths made it easier for them to project their voices.

At Home

Most Greeks were farmers or craftsmen, living in simple houses. Businesses were family-run with a few slaves to help out.

Greek houses were arranged around a courtyard with an altar in the middle. Ordinary Greek houses were made from mud bricks, dried in the sun. It was easy to dig through the walls, so burglars were known as wall-diggers.

The living rooms were on the ground floor, with bedrooms above. Often men and women had separate living areas and spent most of their time apart. Food was cooked over open fires in the kitchen. The smoke escaped through a hole in the roof.

▶ Parts of this house have been cut away, so you can see inside.

▶ Inside a typical Greek house, walls were plain with just a few hangings. Chests were used for storage.

kitchen

alter

living room

herm

Clothes

Men's tunics were made from wool or linen. A plain square of material called a **chiton** was fastened over one or both shoulders and belted around the waist. Women wore a long tunic called a **peplos**, or a long chiton. Wealthier people had tunics made from decorated material, while slaves had plain tunics. In classical times, it was fashionable for men to have short hair and a beard.

Cloaks and shawls would be worn outside in colder weather and for travelling. Many people went barefoot most of the time. Shoes were leather sandals or boots.

Although Greek cities always had public baths, there was no soap, so the Greeks rubbed their bodies with olive oil to get clean. Then they would scrape the oil and dirt off with a tool called a **strigil**.

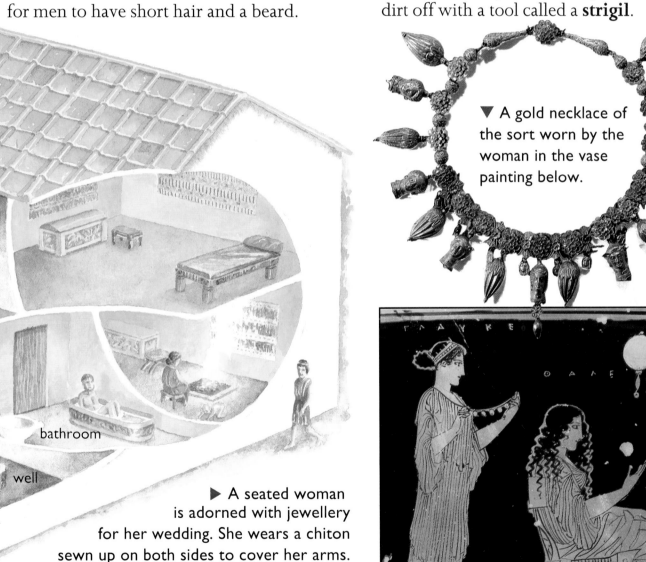

bathroom

well

▼ A gold necklace of the sort worn by the woman in the vase painting below.

▶ A seated woman is adorned with jewellery for her wedding. She wears a chiton sewn up on both sides to cover her arms.

◀ At the front of most houses stood a statue of the god Hermes, a **herm**, thought to act as a guard for the house.

Food

The ancient Greek diet was simple and very healthy. The Greeks ate bread, cheese, fruit, vegetables, eggs, and not much meat. Only wealthy people could afford to eat meat often. Many Greeks lived near the sea, so fish and seafood were very popular.

Farmers grew wheat, barley, grapes and olives. Grapes were eaten or made into wine. Olives were pressed for their oil which was used for cooking, lighting and cleaning. Some farmers kept animals such as pigs, sheep and goats. Bees were kept for honey. Vegetables such as peas, beans, turnips, garlic and onions were also grown, and such fruit as pomegranates, dates, figs and melons.

Breakfast and lunch were small meals, and the main meal was in the evening. Often the Greeks held big dinner parties. Only men were invited and they would sit on couches, eating several courses and drinking lots of wine. After the meal, the men would stay to drink and have a discussion at a **symposium**, or drinking party.

▲ This vase painting shows the messenger of the gods bringing humanity the gift of grain.

Pomegranates

Figs

Fresh dates

Olives

Dried dates

20

Greek Sweetmeats

The Greeks ate **sweetmeats,** made from dates, figs, nuts, sesame seeds and honey, between courses at a symposium, or as little snacks. Here are some for you to make.

Put 100g of sesame seeds into a saucepan with 4 large tablespoons of honey. Ask an adult to help you simmer the mixture over a low heat for 10-20 minutes, until it is a rich gold colour. You can tell if it is ready by dropping a spoonful on a wet plate, letting it cool, then working it into a ball. If it keeps its shape, it is ready. Take the pan off the heat and stir the mixture every few minutes until it is almost cold. Wet your hands with cold water and roll spoonfuls of the mixture into 20-25 little balls. Wrap each sweetmeat in greaseproof paper.

Grapes

Arts and Crafts

The Greeks thought that there was a perfect shape for any object whether it was a simple clay pot or a huge temple. They used both mathematics and **aesthetics,** ideas about what is good in art, to try to make their art as beautiful as possible.

▲ The Greeks made elegant pots covered in patterns and paintings. Many were used every day, for storing water, oil, or wine, but some of the most beautiful pots were carefully saved and then buried with the dead.

◄ Greek statues were made from stone or bronze. Early statues were not lifelike, but as the skills of the sculptors developed, they became graceful, with expressive faces and clothes which looked real. Most stone statues were painted, but have now lost their colour.

▶ The Parthenon in Athens is one of the finest ancient Greek buildings still standing. It is made from carved blocks of cream-coloured marble, held together with wooden pegs and metal clamps. Each side is decorated with rows of columns, typical of Greek architecture. This classical style has been copied all over the world. Is there a building like this near where you live?

Bronze Statues

Bronze statues were made with the 'lost wax' method.

▼ When the clay was finally removed, a bronze statue was revealed.

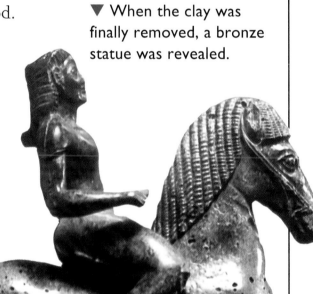

First, a clay model was made, and wooden pegs were stuck into it. Then the clay model was covered with a thin layer of wax. The details of the statue's face and clothes were then sculpted into the wax.

The model was covered with clay and heated so the wax melted and ran out. Molten bronze was poured between the clay layers.

Growing Up

Greek boys went to school from the age of 7 to 15. Fees were charged, so usually boys from poorer families did not stay at school for long. Girls were taught to look after the house, spin and weave by their mothers.

In Athens and many other cities, boys learned reading, writing and math, as well as music, poetry and sport.

In Sparta, life was much harder. If babies were weak or ill, they were left to die on a hillside. Boys were taught to be tough, to prepare them for their life as soldiers. At the age of seven, they were sent away to a strict boarding school. They had no sandals or warm clothes and had to sleep on the hard ground. They were left hungry and had to steal and hunt for their own food. They were beaten and taught to fight and use soldiers' weapons.

◀ This baby's bottle would have been fitted with a leather or cloth teat.

▶ A child's terracotta doll, with jointed arms and legs.

The Greek Alphabet

Some Greek letters are quite similar to those we use today. You may have heard some of their names before. Do you know where our word 'alphabet' comes from?

Greek letter	Name	English sound		Greek letter	Name	English sound		Greek letter	Name	English sound		Greek letter	Name	English sound
A α	alpha	a		H η	eta	ey		N ν	nu	n		T τ	tau	t
B β	beta	b		Θ θ	theta	th		Ξ ξ	xi	ks		Y υ	upsilon	u
Γ γ	gamma	g		I ι	iota	i		O o	omicron	o		Φ φ	phi	ph
Δ δ	delta	d		K κ	kappa	k		Π π	pi	p		X χ	chi	ch
E ε	epsilon	e		Λ λ	lambda	l		P ρ	rho	r		Ψ ψ	psi	ps
Z ζ	zeta	z		M μ	mu	m		Σ σ,ς	sigma	s		Ω ω	omega	oh

Theseus and the Minotaur

*The ancient Greeks told many tales, or myths, about their gods and about the world around them.
Myths often included real events from Greek history. This tale recalls a time long ago when
Greece was dominated by the island of Crete, and Athens was not yet a powerful city state.
It tells the story of the hero Theseus, who overcame the Minotaur,
a terrifying beast which was half man and half bull.*

Athenians trembled at the very mention of Crete. The name 'Minotaur' was enough to make even the bravest man shiver. Every nine years, King Minos of Crete demanded a terrible tribute from the Athenians. Seven young men and seven young women had to be sent to Crete to be fed to the fearsome Minotaur. A ship with black sails would come to Athens each time the tribute was due. As the ship sailed, a huge crowd would gather at the harbour, weeping and wailing.

In Crete, the prisoners were guests of honour at a huge banquet. They were given fine clothes, and offered the most delicious food. Few of them could eat. Afterwards, they were shut in a large room filled with every possible luxury, but few could sleep.

The next day, they were taken to wooden doors, carved with pictures of galloping bulls. From behind came a loud bellowing and stamping. The doors opened and a prisoner was pushed through.

The small crowd of prisoners, guards and priestesses waited until they heard a blood-curdling scream. Then a priestess would point to the next prisoner to be sent through the doors. This went on until the prisoners had all met their fate. Then the Athenians could rest easy for nine years, until it was time to make another tribute.

One year, young Theseus was among the people sent as a tribute to Crete. He, unlike the other prisoners, sat dry-eyed on the ship. He laughed and chatted as they prepared for the banquet, until the others began to feel quite cheerful too. At the banquet, he sat near King Minos's daughter Ariadne, who was charmed by this handsome and brave young man. All evening, they sat and talked.

Ariadne told Theseus that behind the doors there was an elaborate maze. Innumerable paths twisted and turned, confusing the eye and the mind. A person entering the maze could never find their way out.

In the very heart of the maze, there lived the Minotaur. He knew all the twists and turns and blind alleys. If someone stumbled into the maze, the Minotaur would find him or her within moments.

Ariadne was determined to help the brave Theseus. After the banquet, she crept into the sleeping chamber and called softly to Theseus. All his weapons had been taken away, but Ariadne handed him a sword. Then she led the way to the great carved wooden door of the maze.

"Here I must wait for you," she said, and she handed Theseus a ball of thread.

"What is this for?" Theseus said, puzzled.

"As you walk through the maze, unwind this thread behind you. If you succeed, you can follow the thread back. The Minotaur will be asleep, so creep silently through the passages until you reach his lair. With surprise on your side, you may beat him."

Theseus took the thread from Ariadne and pushed open the great door. He stepped inside and closed the door, trapping the end of the thread in the crack. Then, holding his sword in front of him and letting out the thread as he went, Theseus headed into the puzzling maze. He could hear the snores of the Minotaur, and set off toward the noise. A few minutes later, however, he could hardly hear the noise. The path had doubled back, and he was now further away from the centre than when he had started. Theseus pulled in the thread and followed it back to the last place where there had been a choice of paths.

"If I take a path which seems to lead toward the Minotaur, I end up farther away," he said to himself. "So, if I choose a path which leads away, I will eventually reach the Minotaur."

So Theseus set off, creeping quietly along a path which appeared to lead away from the Minotaur's snores. Suddenly, he found himself stumbling into the mouth of a dark cave. From inside, he heard a huge roar, followed by the sound of heavy footsteps. The Minotaur appeared in the entrance.

Theseus gasped and dropped his sword. The Minotaur was even more terrifying than he had imagined.

It had the body of a huge, strong man, and the head of an angry bull. Theseus picked up his sword, just as the Minotaur leapt forward to grab him. He struck the Minotaur a mighty blow on the leg. The Minotaur was not used to people fighting back. Most of his victims were prisoners who had no weapons. Within a few minutes, Theseus had struck a final blow and the Minotaur lay dead at his feet.

Picking up the end of Ariadne's thread, he retraced his steps through the maze to the outer door. Ariadne was waiting for him.

"Quick," she whispered, "We must hurry. Once my father finds out, he will send all the guards to look for us."

Theseus and Ariadne hurried back to the room where the prisoners were held and told them what had happened. Ariadne distracted the guard while the prisoners slipped out. Then she led them all down to the harbour. They set sail for Athens just as the alarm was raised in the palace.

Theseus was proclaimed a hero by the people of Athens who rejoiced that they no longer had to pay the terrible tribute to King Minos.

How We Know

Have you ever wondered how we know so much about the Greeks when they lived so many hundreds of years ago?

Evidence from the Ground

The Greeks built many buildings and made many beautiful objects. Many of these survive but are buried underground. Archaeologists can dig these up and learn much from them. Pictures on pottery, for example, can represent real scenes.

▲ The painting which decorates this plate shows two Greek heroes fighting over the body of a soldier.

▲ Alexander the Great in a detail from a Roman mosaic showing his battle against the Persian Emperor, Darius. Alexander extended Greek territory as far east as India. He brought Greek ideas and customs to all the countries he conquered.

Evidence from Books

The Greeks kept records of all sortsof things, from history and philosophy to lists of goods in stores. Many of these survive, or copies of them do. They tell us all about the Greeks and their lives.

Evidence around Us

Many Greek buildings still stand today as evidence of the skill of Greek builders and architects. Also most European languages have words which were originally Greek, especially words connected with the arts, such as 'drama' and scientific words such as 'psychology' and 'astronomy'.

▲ The Theseus temple still stands in Athens.

Glossary

aesthetics
Ideas about what is good in art. The Greeks believed that balance and symmetry were very important in art.

chiton
A simple tunic worn by men and women.

citizen
A citizen was a man who had the right to own property and take part in politics and law.

democracy
A political system involving government by citizens. In Greece, only men with property were entitled to be citizens, with the right to vote on matters of government.

herm
A small statue which stood outside the door of a house to protect the household.

Mount Olympus
The mountain in Greece where the gods were thought to live.

oracle
A holy place where the gods could be asked questions with the help of a priest or priestess.

ostraka
A pottery fragment on which citizens wrote the names of those they wished to banish from the city.

peplos
A long tunic worn by women only.

philosopher
A person who studied the world about them. In Greece, all great thinkers were known as philosophers.

polis
A state consisting of a city and the surrounding countryside.

sacrifice
An offering made to a god to bring good fortune or to ask the god not to be angry.

slave
A worker who was owned by a citizen. Slaves had few rights, but they could buy their freedom if they saved enough money.

strigil
A curved blade usually of metal used for scraping oil and dirt from the skin.

soothsayer
A person who could predict the future and tell fortunes.

sweetmeats
A small sweet snack often made from preserved fruit or nuts.

symposium
A drinking party, where discussions were held, and entertainments may have taken place.

Index